Lessons from The Park

Robert Dusek

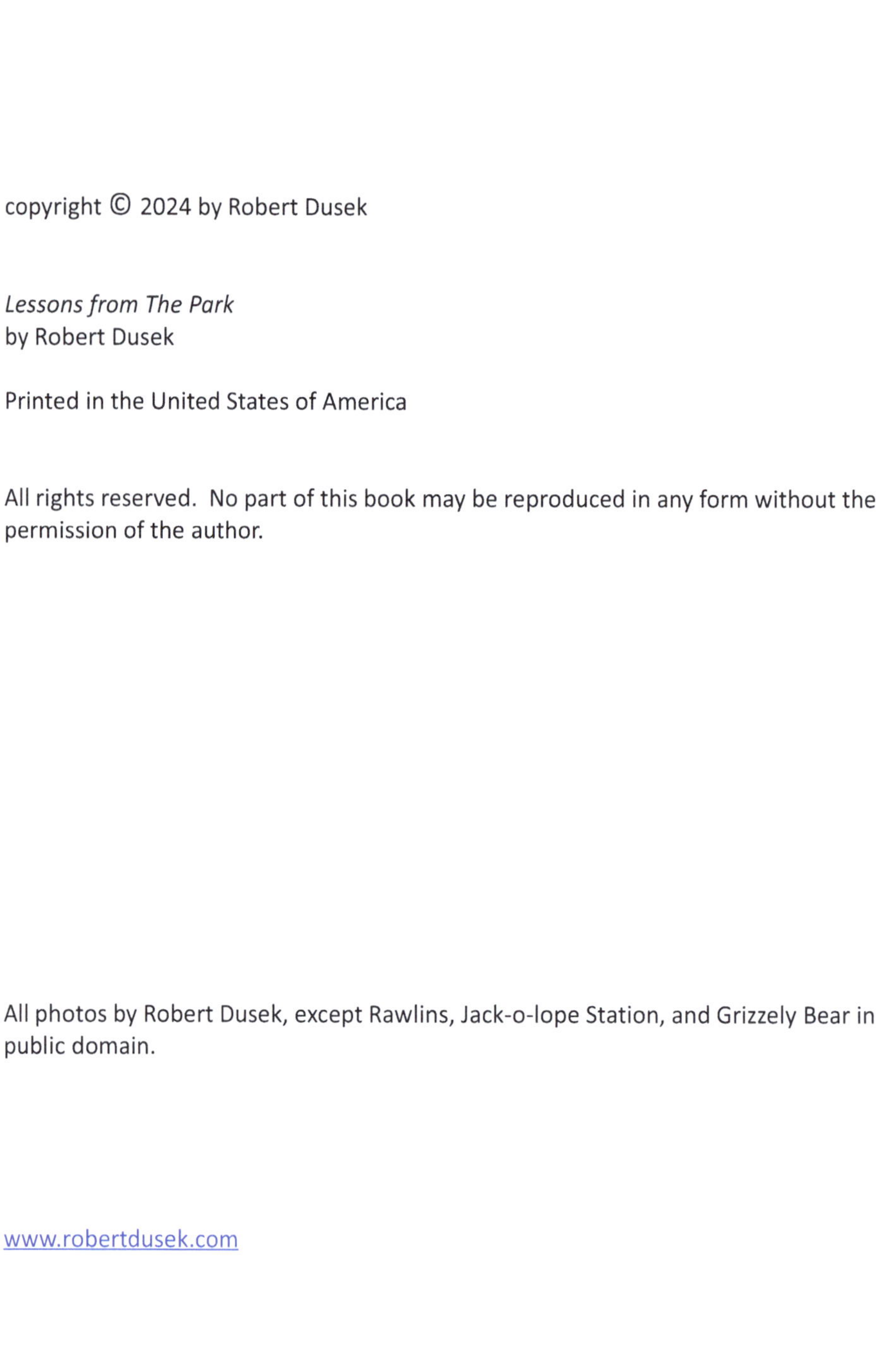

to all who frequent Wonderland...

And softly dripping, drop by drop,
Upon the quiet mountaintop,
Steals drowsily and musically
Into the universal valley.

- Edgar Allan Poe

Lessons from the Park

Listening for Whispers

Lessons - life lessons, business lessons, leadership lessons - are learned in a variety of classrooms. The school classroom, the playground, the relationship classroom, the business meeting; all impart their own kind of wisdom and guidance if one consciously seeks.

For me, the outdoors has proven to be the storehouse of leadership and life lessons. When one gets away from the daily grind, one has time and space to reflect upon seemingly uneventful happenings to find the extraordinary in the mundane. And for me there has been no greater teacher than Yellowstone National Park. Existing as it does at the confluence of civilization and vast wilderness, it offers unique insight into this experience we call life. If we are quiet enough to listen.

Octopus Spring, a place of solitude

I

The trip to Yellowstone National Park is a fascinating undertaking. Driving from my home near Denver to Old Faithful takes about 12 hours. Traveling alone, I begin my journey wondering just why I should embark on such a trek. I pop a CD in the dashboard player and listen to a symphony or two before my first stop on the border between Colorado and Wyoming. Inquisitive of my own sanity - why should anyone desire to drive this lonely route? - I purpose to trod on.

Travel

About four hours into the drive, I stop at a restaurant in Rawlins, the proud home of the famous two story outhouse. The scenery had since changed from moderate steppe to dry rocks and gravel - the wind, whipping up the sand and dust. I once again question my sanity, but this would be the last time. Driving north out of town, the surroundings become more varied and wonderful. A straight shot across the Great Divide Basin in the Red Desert where water flows neither east nor west, a paralleling of the Mormon trail with its historic landmarks, and an exciting descent into the Wind River valley with its exquisitely colored sandstone and deep blue rapids. By the time I arrive at Dubois for the final gasoline fill-up at the "Jack-o-lope" station, I know that the drive to Yellowstone is not only sane, but an exciting trek into one of life's most wonderful experiences.

The Jackolope Station in Dubois

What surprises me to this day is that while I have driven this route many times, it continues to present the same mental challenges: An initial hesitation - a question of whether it will be worth it - followed by a gradual transition period where doubts are shed, finally culminating in an exuberance over the magnificence of the long lonely drive itself. Its as if there exists a need to spend some time putting the starting point behind, leaving that which is comfortable day in and day out, even questioning the worthiness of the journey before getting to that place where I can embrace the wonders of the road ahead.

the Grand Tetons on the way to "The Park"

The journey from Dubois to The Park* is nothing short of spectacular. One is treated to mountain passes, views of the Grand Tetons, and a beautiful drive along Jackson Lake. After climbing the rim of the Yellowstone Caldera and entering The Park, the drive traverses the rim of the Lewis River Canyon, past the beautifully set Lewis Falls, along the shore of its name-sake lake, all before descending to the edge of the inland ocean known as Yellowstone Lake with it's unique lake-shore thermal features. After crossing the continental divide twice, one finally arrives at the Upper Geyser Basin, home to the greatest collect-

---

*Yellowstone regulars refer to Yellowstone as "The Park." While there are many national parks in the U.S., there is only one that is "The Park."

ion of Geysers on earth and the famous Old Faithful. Most people park in the Old Faithful parking lot, but I always make it a point to head to the Lower Hamilton Store parking area as it is right next to the boardwalks and a bit away from the madness that is the throng of tourists.

There is a routine I generally follow before seeking evening accommodations. I will walk the basin boardwalks, connect with some of the regular *gazers*, and head to the Old Faithful Inn to consume an elk-burger and maybe a vodka gimlet. If Martha is

providing the live music, I say hello and maybe we play a couple of duets.

And my arrival in Yellowstone is just the beginning of the magical discovery. But no matter how many times I travel to this Wonderland, I begin by second guessing myself: Should I really be making this trip? Will it be worth it? How much cost or inconvenience will I incur?   I have found that those questions can only be answered *after* the journey has begun. Maybe not until the journey is complete. One must shed the present day-to-day routine, and only after the perspective has changed and a new vista experienced can one evaluate the validity of the journey. Is it possible to truly examine that which has not yet been experienced? And just because one experiences the journey once doesn't mean that reminding is not important. For some reason my travels to the Park always begin with what is later shown to be irrelevant questions.

When you have arrived, you will be in a different place - not only physically, but mentally, spiritually, emotionally. And you will realize that arriving only begins the journey afresh. Don't let the concerns and questions you may have before embarking keep you from traveling the road before you.

a different kind of place

firehole river

II

There is a grand old geyser near the northern edge of the Upper Geyser Basin called Artemesia. Named for the gray-green color of its sagebrush-resembling geyserite deposits, it is a massive beautiful pool when not erupting. It sits below an overlook on the foot trail that used to be the old road through the basin. It's a picturesque setting and I like to hang out here just to slow down and maybe get a good sun burn.

Artemisia
The eruptions of Artemisia are proceeded by a thumping in the ground as steam bubbles form and collapse. Then the massive pool sends forth bursts of water some thirty feet in the air for fifteen to thirty minutes. Often the show is veiled in steam, but when the breeze is favorable, the spectacle is unlike any other.

Unfortunately, Artemisia is technically unpredictable. Its intervals (times between eruptions) have ranged from 5 hours to over 3 days, probably longer, and while there have been seasons when it has been more regular than others, averaging maybe 14 or 20 hours between eruptions, it has never been predicted with any sort of certainty, and what is discovered one season often changes with the passing of years.

Artemisia during its quiet interval

On a trip to the Park in 2012, I thought I had Artemisia "figured out." I had seen dozens of eruptions over the years and had noticed that there were slight variations in the gas bubbles issuing from its various vents prior to an eruption. They became larger and more numerous, specifically from the far vent, approximately 30-40 minutes before an eruption. I wasn't certain of the find, but had tested it on several occasions and the methodology held. I was getting good at predicting Artemisia. I was about to learn a lesson about predictions.

One day, a woman and her daughter began hiking toward Artemisia, and as it was also my destination, we embarked together. The first item of business was to inform them that the safety pin was still in their can of bear spray rendering it inoperable. Having resolved that issues, we arrived at Artemisia to a full pool and numerous large gas bubbles. Although I had invited them to stay for the impending show, they elected to continue on as their schedule did not include a prolonged wait for a possible eruption. I stayed; it certainly couldn't be more than 30 minutes until the show.

About an hour later, another group of hikers arrived, and since the pool was vigorously overflowing while belching its bubbles, I convinced them to stay and wait. And wait we did. After about two hours they left. I stayed another hour or so, crossing paths again with the woman and her daughter who were surprised to find me still in place. After yet another hour I finally left. It was getting dark and I was getting hungry. I retreated with a severe sunburn and the horrible feeling that comes from having convinced people to give up hours of their time, based upon my "methodology." To wait for an event that never happened. I felt bad, having imposed my error on those who trusted in my so-called "learned judgment."

In retrospect, there was nothing wrong with my judgment. It was based upon observation and confirmed through repetition. The knowledge was all there, but the wisdom was not. There are sayings among geyser gazers which I shall summarize: "It's a geyser. It doesn't care about your predictions. It will erupt when it erupts." Or as gazer Jim once put it, "when all these things happen, there's a *possibility* that an eruption *might* occur."

Knowledge may predicts things. Wisdom tempers those predictions with realism. It is wise to know that the future is not certain, that it is not one hundred percent predictable. Better to say that we *look* for outcomes based upon our observations than to predict those outcomes with certainty. Never promise that which is outside your ability to deliver.

lower geyser basin river wonders

III

Mud Pots

An area in the Lower Geyser Basin of Yellowstone National Parks contains some of the parks best mud pots - mud that boils and blurbs at the surface due to the water and steam beneath. [Imagine a pot of thick pea soup boiling on the stove, transpose and recolor that image to fill in pockets of land within a substantial expanse and you have the idea.] These mud pots are off the beaten track and not frequently visited, especially recently since rangers have started patrolling the area to keep tourists away - for their own supposed safety.

I shan't reveal the exact location of these mud pots, but suffice it to say that I was in search of an area called Microcosm Basin and took a wrong turn. I was advised to seek this unique basin as it was something unlike anything else in the Park. I prepared for the journey in advance: water, snacks, camera, first aid, compass, map. As it was a hot day, I was traveling light. No need for overnight gear - this trek would be no longer than a few hours.

I really enjoy hiking the road less traveled by myself, and this excursion was a beautiful experience with some trail following, some off trail exploring, some vistas, a lone bull bison, and a breathtaking view of a few geysers from a perspective not often seen. I must have turned north a bit too soon, so rather than descending into the expected valley of a long extinct explosion crater, I noticed the ground becoming stark, hollow and mostly void of vegetation, except for the dried, dead kind. At some fortuitous moment I decided to halt and test the ground with my walking stick. To my both surprise and dread I found the ground immediately to my left, right and ahead to be hollow. There appeared to be what possibly might be a thin track of solid

ground, but to break through this hollow firmament would be to experience boiling mud first hand. The only sure footing was back the way I came.

Hollow ground, not for crossing

Tracing my steps backwards was to admit defeat; to admit failure. More over, it would keep me out long after sunset, and it's never a good idea to be hiking in the back country alone after dark - did I mention that I was in bear territory? Trudging on might not only be foolish, but fatal.

My decision was made when I struck the ground to my left and it cracked open revealing a boiling cauldron. I would retrace my steps and stay out past dark. This was also the day I would vow to never hike in the back-country without a flashlight - the last mile or so was replete with tripping hazards.

* * *

It's not as much about being prepared, or researching a route, or admitting mistakes, or having the correct timing. It's about knowing when to turn around; to not go forward. It's knowing when to back up and find another way, maybe at another time. No matter how prepared, researched, competent or humble we are, we sometimes find ourselves in places where the only choice is to go back - to regroup.   It is not defeat, it is the beginning of discovering a different solution. It is also safeguarding that which is important.

One of the most difficult lessons to learn is that sometimes "stuff just happens." It's not malicious, nor planned; it's not expected, nor can it be avoided. It is just "stuff." When all the prep work is correctly done, when the journey is well advised, encouraged, mapped out and executed, you might still find yourself stuck in the mud.   In these cases know that the "stuff" happens, and maybe it's just time to back up and find an alternate route.

Castle Geyser, upper geyser basin

IV

Beehive

The Hill. That magnificent elevation of thermal ground across the river from Old Faithful. The home of forty or more intercon-nected geysers - some small and intriguing, some large and breathtaking. The playground of Giantess geyser; the pride of the Lion Complex; Aurum Geyser, Bench, Goggles, and the Ane-nome Geysers. And also the location of the tallest regularly ac-tive cone-type geyser in the world, Beehive. Play from Beehive can exceed 200 feet drenching the nearby boardwalk and it's un-suspecting travelers. The power of its play can be felt as the ground shakes while steam and water escape in high velocity jets.

Although Beehive is not a "predictable" geyser, there exist an adjacent unique feature - Beehive's Indicator - that allows for many to experience the show. It send up a fifteen foot continu-ous column of water shortly before the massive eruption of Bee-hive, serving as a predictor of Beehive's impending deluge.

Whenever I am on The Hill and the "Indicator" begins to shoot forth its gentle and wispy spikes of water, I make it a point to corral the visitors to the impending show, imploring them to wait for what will certainly be the most memorable part of their vacation. Some look at me incredulously. Others are thankful. Some must think me crazy, but most will give fifteen to twenty minutes of their time to see if Beehive will really go off. And dur-ing this time gazers begin to gather and the size of the crowd around the cone increases dramatically.

Then it happens. A particularly large splash heralds the climbing column of water and steam to unbelievable heights, soaking the boardwalk and the unsuspecting viewer. I have never heard anyone complain about waiting for an eruption of Beehive. Contrary, I have witnessed universal appreciation for the one who encourages the throng to stay and wait for the show.

Beehive

* * *

Without one to encourage those to stop and wait, many would walk right by and miss that which is one of the most memorable experiences. When I first began coming to The Park I hesitated to corral those on The Hill for fear that I might be wrong in my "Indicator" informed prediction. However, Beehive is not Artemesia. The indicator is easily recognized and the methodology has been proven over a long period of time. Is it 100% reliable? No, but it's about as close to infallible as one can get when dealing with geysers. And so now I make it a point to "call it" every time. It's about being a blessing to others who might otherwise miss something spectacular.

If you have the opportunity to bless someone or someones, don't withhold your blessing. Share it liberally. You will be thanked. And all will be a bit richer.

V

Yellowstone would not be Yellowstone without the expanse of back-country to experience and explore. And the back-country would not be the back-country without bears.

Bear

Most years one can read about fatal maulings by a grizzly bears upon unsuspecting and ill-prepared tourists. Yes, more people are attacked each year by bison, but there is something extra frightening about a bear encounter. And even packing a container of bear spray doesn't bring much comfort when the bear is in front of you and your bear spray is safely stored away in your back pack.

When heading into the back-country, one should never travel alone. Groups of 4 are preferred since if one is injured, one can stay while two go for help. But even traveling in pairs in fine for observant and circumspect hikers. If you never want to encounter a bear, wear a bell, make some noise and always travel upwind. You won't see a bear, but you also won't see any other wildlife; you will have a noisy and unpleasant experience, the trade-off for being super safe.

Enjoyment in the back-country - the silence and solitude, the wildlife experience, the feeling of renewal - all come with the risk of a close up encounter with a grizzly. I know of no regular visitor to The Park who has not, at one time or another, discovered themselves up close and personal with the great bear.

The thing to remember in such cases is that the bear doesn't want to encounter you just as much as you don't want to encounter him. A slow and careful retreat will almost always de-escilate the encounter and allow each to go their respective paths.

Robert Frost, in his famous poem The Road Not Taken, penned, "Two roads diverged in a wood, and I -- I took the one less traveled by, And that has made all the difference." The road less traveled in The Park is the back-country; the place where silence and wildlife converge, where renewal of perspective is commonplace and adventure is had. It is important to travel this path; it is also important to count the cost and know the way out. There are dangers in any worthwhile endevour - the trick is how to manage those dangers; and that comes from being prepared for the unexpected encounter.

VI

Visitor

Visiting The Park for the first time in an overwhelming experience. Most do not realize how large The Park truly is - almost as large as the state of Connecticut; three times the size of Rhode Island. At over 2.2 million acres, spanning three states, it is a sizable footprint. Yet many still think they can "see The Park" in a day. They are not prepared for the expanse of this area and the amount of time it takes to experience the many "features" of Wonderland.

Opalescent Pool

Visitors are often an endless source of entertainment for Park regulars. I remember encountering a dad explaining to his kids that a geyser wasn't erupting because the managers needed to divert the water elsewhere. One proud intellectual once explained to me how the rangers regulate the water flow to keep the geyser basins open. And so many of the questions one receives would certainly try one patience if it weren't for the fact that they are so whimsical, and even comical: "What time does The Park close?" "What do they do with the animals at night?" "Who schedules the eruptions?" Gazer Tara related a story to me about a group of people who were staying at the Old Faithful Lodge. While in the gift shop they asked her, "where is Old Faithful?" Tara pointed them in the correct direction only to be approached by the same group again. "We still can't find the geyser," they said. "Can you help us." Tara once again explained where they should go to see the grand wonder, and when all was said and done a member of that group received a revelation: "Oh!, you mean the geyser is **outside**!"

These stories are certainly humorous, but for myself, when I hear such fantastic rhetoric, I wish to correct the speaker. "No, sir, The Park doesn't close, and the animals take care of themselves. Eruptions are not scheduled. There are not valves and pipes underneath the surface that the rangers use to divert the water flow! And, yes! The Old Faithful geyser is not a fountain that was erected in your hotel lobby!!" It feels as if I am called to correct misinformation and false beliefs, and those whom I correct should be grateful because I have increased their knowledge base. The only problem is: people don't *like* to be corrected.

The dad explaining to his kids about why a geyser isn't erupting doesn't want to be told that he is wrong in front of his kids, especially by a stranger. The person wondering about Park hours or animal comforts do not want to feel like they are stupid to inquire. Even those looking for Old Faithful in all the wrong places would rather discover the errors of their search themselves than be told that they don't know what they are talking about.

What is needful to be said? When one actively looks for feedback, correction may be welcome; yet it must always be gingerly expressed, especially in public. Pointing out errors should never be the opening of a discourse, regardless of how right you are or how wrong the other might be. There are always more dynamics at work.

The fool speaks because he has to say something.
He feels compelled to right the wrong or to correct the error.

The wise speaks because he has something to say.
He states something needful and not impulsive.

Encouraging a visitor about an impending eruption of Beehive may be needful - an opportunity to share a blessing. Correcting someone's demonstrated ignorance or foolishness is not.

An early morning Old Faithful eruption

VII

Time

Time truly does slow down. When your not concerned about mud pots, or visitors, or the path ahead, you realize that time passes more slowly in the geyser basins. The period is not set to the clock, and the waiting is just part of being. The land breathes on its own time and that is an expanse unconcerned with deadlines and schedules.

Rabbit Creek

To wake early and experience the cold sun slowly rise over the frost bitten land just in time to give way to plumes of boiling water is to bring oneself to an altogether different place. To wonder at the bright display of the Milky Way stretching across the heavens where no light can dim its banner is to see nightfall for the first time. Sitting alone in the darkness waiting for an eruption of Grand to the music of coyotes and owls elevates the senses in uncommon ways; better yet to spend the night in the back-country in the haunt of the great bear.

And while time passes, ones perception of time evaporates into the simple essence of being, where we are not concerned with what comes next - only with what is. Time spent in The Park is really not time spent, it is time ignored - for a time. If it were only possible to transplant this experience to our daily lives so that we might live in the presence without the pressures of an unknown future or unfulfilled past. Maybe then we could live worthy of this gift we call life.

Ice Lake

Reflection

It's been said that a journey of a thousand miles begins with a single step. That step is not simply a step forward, but a step away from the past, from the comfortable. Its the beginning of an amazing journey forward that you never realized you needed until you have walked the path. Too many stay home in the day to day cage of comfort, never experiencing the very life they are blessed with because they never justified taking that first step, making that correct choice. Yet it is in the wonder of arrival in that "other place" where we meditate, learn, reflect and grow.

For me, The Park will always be that place where perspective is allowed to influence my life. May you find your "park" and may you visit it often.

Robert Dusek first visited The Park in 1997, and from that point forward he was hooked.   Regularly returning, he has developed a great appreciation for the revitalization The Park offers to those who take the time to experience its wonders, reflect on its nature, and listen to its whispers.